Ruination

Katie Jean Shinkle

SPUYTEN DUYVIL
NEW YORK CITY

Acknowledgements

Endless gratitude and appreciation to Tod Thilleman and Spuyten Duyvil for the hard work and dedication to seeing my vision and championing it, as well as for being such a beautiful and important publishing institution.

To the following publications where parts of this work first appeared, sometimes largely in different forms: *LIT Magazine*, *Ninth Letter*, and *Washington Square Review*.

And, last but not least, to the early readers and supporters of this work, who offered love, advice, and editing: Pj Carlisle, Julia Cohen, Patty Yumi Cottrell, Meghan L. Dowling, Steven Dunn, Lily Hoang; and to these amazing artists for their generous blurbs: Steven Dunn, Patty Yumi Cottrell, Andrea Lawlor, and Scott McClanahan.

©2018 Katie Jean Shinkle
ISBN 978-1-947980-41-9

Cover photo by Amith Nair on Unsplash (@a_myth)
Interior photo by Joel Peel on Unsplash (@joel_m_peel)

Library of Congress Cataloging-in-Publication Data

Names: Shinkle, Katie Jean.
Title: Ruination / Katie Jean Shinkle.
Description: New York : Spuyten Duyvil, [2018]
Identifiers: LCCN 2018002269 | ISBN 9781947980419
Classification: LCC PS3619.H5766 R85 2018 | DDC 813/.6--dc23
LC record available at https://lccn.loc.gov/2018002269

For Pj Carlisle

I.

The Slayer, Time

::

Reckoning: An Atmospheric Condition Like Ours

::

Vegetative Girl Ruin

Darkness, and then. Rolling weather: a superstorm in-wait. Four clouds exactly alike, black outline as if spiral on paper. Stratus or cirrus. Paredolia in theory: what becomes a creature of wing, what becomes one blink signal or two, what becomes the shape of genitals. If we take our shoes off, put them behind our heads, lie on our backs, can we stay like this forever, pointing at creatures and penises in the sky, the largest span of blackbird ever seen?

Can we begin in the war of this country in the summer of us? Paula, Allison, Callie, & I all wear black swimming caps, swim in syncopation, a rising chorus of legs, arm-in-arm, splash.

Before the weather, before the war, us four girls will huddle around the computer and watch videos of syncopated swimming routines. Face down in the carpet, we will emulate moves. We will begin to touch each other, first on the legs and then up under the shorts, the mesh entangling with our chipped gel manicures. The videos shift from film clips of Esther Williams to porn clips with titles like "He takes it real good 2" and "Busty Brazilian Luvs Anal." The touching of butts will lead to flashing breasts, comparing, poking at Paula's because they are slightly pancakey, wobbly.

All the light of day is muted by fog, blocking the summer sun, no matter the time. The only light for miles at night comes from the revival tent, a man who calls himself The Prophet. A local transient, until now. All The Men are desperate. They need faith and hope. They will take it wherever they can get it. *Holy, holy, holy, God almighty, bless-ed trinity.* The only thing I believe in is the Holy Spirit because I have seen it. I have seen it when my father puts on a lacy dress, a choke chain, high heels, struts around the house like the Queen of the World. Miles of corn and soybeans and my father in a chevron skirt, blue eyeshadow, fake lashes so long. I have seen the transformation alight on his face; *when my father is dressed like a woman he is the closest he will ever be to God*, I tell Paula.

My father says *I truly feel like myself in women's clothing, but I am not a woman.* He says dressing in women's clothing has always been a secret, something my mother never understood about him.

We prepare for the superstorm in the following ways: catching rain in the cups of our goblet-hands, laced with gold lamé. We put our goblet-hands under the muted fog and save a cache of rainbow spectrum for later. Our hands become hammers and we board up the windows, nails falling from the trees like fruits. Writing in spray paint on the sides of the houses, we predict the outcome. The colors of paint, the numbers and symbols translate: one alive, two dead, dog in here, zero crossed out one crossed out two crossed out three, PLZ HELP. Paula and I huddle in the basement behind a twin mattress. My father is in Eastern Village. We do not know Eastern Village no longer exists yet. The sky turns grey to green to greener than I have ever seen.

After, in-between, preceding, prolouging, eulogizing, the superstorm is here. Instructions: go to a safe place, if one exists at all in the world. Cover your head. Do not leave. Do not stay. Do not drive. Do not be frozen adjacent to your largest window. Emergency Broadcast: This is only a test of your circulatory system, of your life force thumping against the middle of your forehead. The sky of my heart is a bottle shimmering, the color of beach glass. Ecstatic noise and then not. What angels. How the sky parts the muted sun.

The temperature drops from 80 degrees to 35 degrees in a matter of one hour. Air made of inescapable, damp humidity. Paula and I watch the mini-swirled cyclones skipping around each other, twisting at the base like two heads of the same monster, tunneling and dying.

And then the threatening and ominous heavens like wet paint, dripping, leak and smear, of what will stay in the stratosphere and troposphere, it is July, ashy and freezing.

One hour before, Paula and I pulled the mattress out onto the lawn and held each other as it started to rain. Our hands are soft feathers caressing and I am touching her hips, stomach, tracing the outline of her Tasmanian Devil tattoo. I am down above her underwear line but not over it. The mattress starts stinking from the moisture, and it feels as if there is no one else in the entire world. When we kiss, her long dark hair gets into my mouth. We pull and push each other. Our movement gets so rough that eventually she lands in mud. We laugh until we realize every single lawn is flooded, the street below is waist-high water, cars floating and hitting the sides of trees, everyone evacuated but us.

Later, houses plucked, gone like rotten eyeteeth. That's how weather is, it can't be trusted.

(Confirmed: Eastern Village is no longer a place. Eastern Village is wiped off the map.)

The unliftable fog. It enters, blocks the sun. The rain, then snow, kills everything.

The Men talk of crops. The Men talk of the unlifted fog. The Men talk of 1816, the year of No Summer, the devastation. From here to the UK and back again, The Men say, famine. The Men talk of war, how in the middle of the summerwinter aftermath all women must ship out, sail out, fly out, drive out, get out. The Women are sent to war. Fight for our freedom. The Men talk of the first folded flag to be delivered by hand to a husband already. The Men talk of death and how swift it comes, the grief of having to raise children alone. The Men take off their snapback trucker hats and roll the bills in their scarred hands. The Men fret over food and children, fret over the flowers that they have all seen but will not speak of out loud yet. The Men talk of going elsewhere, to Atlanta or New Orleans, or to Ohio, Iowa, as far west as Missouri, maybe even Colorado, who knows. *That there's the Wild West now, son*, one says to the other, and The Men laugh. Anything with the word wild is scary. When The Men are scared, they engage in violence. Violence against the potential wild. So maybe not Colorado, or anywhere further West. The Men talk of their daughter's synchronized swimming practices, will they still be able to compete if it is so cold? The Men speak of frost, and then of snow, in July, August. The Men are scared of snow, of fog not dissipated, of a rebuild, of where Eastern Village has gone to, of all of the deaths and destruction and the women and the flowers. The Men don't cry, so they hit their bodies with their own fists, waiting for someone else to hit.

The Oldest Men talk of the year 1816, the year of No Summer. Volcanic winter. 1816, an atmospheric condition like ours. *Radioactive fog*, one man says and the other says, *no, volcanoes are not radioactive*.

The Prophet stands before the lean congregation in the heavy, canvas tent, leftovers from a circus fire a town over, charred at the top where a flag should be undulating. Instead, a burnt-out hole. Everyone simultaneously cold and sweating.

Alleluia, Hallelujah, Amen. Brothers! the Prophet says, *This summer-winter is a gift of reclaimation for us from God. We are men! Men of God!* Some of The Men take their pork pie hats off and hold them to their chests by their tops, watching the snow fall through the burnt-out hole.

The Prophet laughs. *Brothers! Our women are at war! Tell me how you will be a man in their absence. Brothers! We are men of the highest order. We must protect our homeland, our nation, one nation under God, remember,* he laughs again, this time it is so high pitched it makes my father wince.

My father joins the relief effort because that's what he thinks he needs to do. He spends his days hauling trees off of houses and rescuing dogs. I watch him across the street one day shaking a chainsaw towards the road while giving directions because he can't seem to stop talking with his hands. He is talking to a member of the National Guard, an 18-year-old with an automatic weapon strapped to his back. My father's gestures with the chainsaw makes the kid nervous. He looks so small compared to my father, who is a massive conglomeration of chest and shoulders, neck and arms. My father revvs the chainsaw and stops talking to the kid, who still looks confused. When my father bends over, I can see the lacy ruffle top of his pink striped underwear.

Paula says *the real enemy, the real terrorist, is time.* A wall of clocks all set incorrectly. Late summer and snow. One meteor length, far and wide. Sideshow, in a specimen jar, bell box. Lift for cake. Lift for sick sweet of rotten coconut, a jelly filling. Our hands against the glass and panting. Shelves of missing. One dough arm, one severed gingersnap head. Forgotten buttons down an abdomen never covered. Abandoned houses. Rush, and a smash of window. The children take lead bats to the framework. Blast of weather, and then silence. Blast, and then a light ash film smog on everything. Make a peace sign in the window with your finger. Someone else writes fuck your mom underneath it.

And fuck your mom might be right. As of today, the last of the mothers are relinquished, and moved at once. Lines of ponytails marching one step two step, stomp. A colonel, as tall as a 10-year-old, told our fathers our mothers must go. No choices. Although they are gone, in the ghostly hours, our mothers still hang in the air, black spirits in the corners of rooms, talons clawing the nautical themed wallpaper. They move fast, backwards and forwards, over the fridge and the kitchen counters. We watch them sizzle their tongues against our fathers' ears and they scratch and bat as if something inside is attempting escape.

The day our mothers leave, Paula wears a Canadian flag pin on her lapel instead of the American flag pin her mother gave her to wear. My mother leans down to kiss me good-bye. Paula's mother does not kiss her. We stand on the lawn and wave at the bus. Our mothers do not wave back.

On the brink of war, and then war. *Do not be sad*, my father says to me. *Your mother will come back.* Watching the river that cuts through town move rapidly, the air changing shape with the same rapidity, my heart races. It will be years until a fast paced stillness doesn't scare me. In the aftermath. In the aftermath, sure and steady, *we are lucky we are here* says Paula's dad, but I can't help but imagine if we would be better off not here, too.

I kiss the outside of Paula's collarbone and she turns her back to me. *We aren't anything you know, you are my best friend*, she says. I lie back down, my arm behind my head. How to stretch, how to breathe. Count back from 100 into perpetuity. Repeat pi digits. Visualization. Behavior Modification. We always think we mistake a slight breeze for breath or fan. Hot air. What gives. I turn my back to Paula, but leave my hand out behind me just in case she wants it to touch her back in the night. No sound outside, no insects or bird calls. The trees are turning brown and leaves are falling prematurely. They believe it is different months other than July and August.

The Prophet says *do you hear me, are you listening, if you are listening say Amen.*

The Men say *Amen.*

The Prophet says *as the Lord as thy witness the last days are here upon us. Upon Us! The last days. Brothers, go with me now to the Book of John—*
For God so Loved the World...

The services run continually. The Prophet speaks so many times a day. He is convinced this situation is not simply a disaster, but an apocalypse, an end of days.

The Prophet sings a hymn from memory with his eyes closed, right hand to the ceiling, left hand on his chest. He has a tattoo of a red-haired, half-naked woman on his left upper arm. He never rolls his sleeves up past his elbow, never wears a white dress shirt without a short sleeved undershirt, but sometimes you can make out the end of stilettos with heels so sharp they could kill.

The Prophet begins to sing *O Come O Come Emmanuel.* Christmas music amongst summerwinter devastation. *And ransom captive Israel.*

After the eight o'clock revival, my father confesses to wearing panties under his Carhartt coveralls full time, but I already know.

First Reports (official):

Female, 12-years-old. Vegetation: Hawaiian Hibiscus. Location: Left and Right Axilla (Armpits).

Female, 15-years-old. Vegetation: American Dogwood. Location: Humerus (upper arm bone).

Female, 8-years-old. Vegetation: White Pine Cone and Tassel: Location: Left Anterior Cruciate Ligament (ACL).

Our Friend Jetta Jackson. Vegetation: Rose (pink, red); Virginia Bluebells. Location: Entire Body.

Our Friend Jetta Jackson is one of the first to be found in bed, rosebuds streaming out of her mouth onto the pillowcase and floor as if her body is filled with them, thick wooden sprawl from her sternum, fingers and veins of aerial roots like toes, a type of plant perception of depth and girth, how far and where could they go, down her soft pudgy stomach to the top of her vagina and in. Brown roots out of her body and into the mattress where they seemingly go on forever, down into the carpet, across the ceiling. In her eyes, two stems of Virginia Bluebells, more purple in hue. Her eyeballs are never recovered.

Our Friend Jetta Jackson's house is engulfed overnight. Vegetation bursts through the siding, pulsating, like the time Jetta's family visited Mexico and got lost. An old couple let them use an outhouse, and when Jetta looked at the walls there were so many lizards moving it looked as if the walls were breathing. Optical Illusion.

The Men attempt to cut the layers.

They are unsuccessful.

We had no idea flowers could grow at such a rate. Check one, check two. Stairs, under or over, above in attic spaces and in basements, where ghosts reside. Here instead of insulation, a wall of violets, thick as if hay and braided, eight by eight. The Men start checking their girls, their houses, every morning, every evening since Our Friend Jetta Jackson. The violet wall carpet cover, entanglement of stalks and bud. Thousands of blooms or mid-corpse expiration petals, half-ripped, whole ripped, deadhead.

My father finds the first sign of Queen Anne's Lace underneath an earthy patch under the carpet in my bedroom. He pulls the hard stalks out, rubs his hands raw. He shakes the small white floral bunches from his sleeves of his shirt at the revival tent that night.

Everyday that there is nothing is a better day than the last. One day there is nothing but carpet and wood floors and ugly bathroom tile and for many days this is the case, carpet, wood floors, ugly bathroom tile. The following day there is a root behind the wall, bulging like a vein. The Men decide when the daughters are at school that they will take a sledgehammer to the plaster and cut the thing out. Everyday after, they check the hole until there is something new: a bulge, larger than the first, reaching the entire length of the hallway, stopping only at the doorframe of a daughter's bedroom. As The Men leave the house, shaking their heads, mumbling phrases like "load bearing" and "structural integrity" they notice all the doorknobs have turned into branch-like strands of Day-Glo orange flowers, fully bloomed.

Even before the superstorm, all of our older sisters are deemed terrorists. My older sister shot a boy in the cheek but the cheek fat lodged the bullet so it did not kill him. The surgeon told the boy he should be happy for all the fat, the bullet could have blown through his face, cheek to cheek. All the boys our sisters chase after are rapists. *They should be happy we don't kill them all dead*, they tell us. Paula's older sister pointed a gun straight at the tip of a boy's dick and fired. The bullet hit his leg, nicked a ball. The older girls with their short hair and cold stares. The older girls who have merely delayed their recon mission until everything returns to normal.

Paula's older sister is found with a hollyhock at the top of her head. The Men lift the stalk from her crown and they are surprised when her entire body moves with it, a fusion.

The vegetation swallows our terrorist older sisters. Once Paula's older sister is found with the hollyhock, her little sister is sent to Indiana. Paula's father leaves the country. *People need to know our girls are dying*, he tells the BBC before flying to Paris. Paula's father is a diplomat. Paula's father feels that his voice will bring international attention. But no one listens. He says, wide-eyed, his hair unwieldy, *Our girls are dying in flowers*.

Paula's father is silenced. His life is threatened. On TV, on talk radio, he says, *this is what is happening and what are you going to do about it*? In Paris on Rue Cler, in front of everyone's cameras, in a cross-legged position, he sets himself on fire. Live footage of Paula's father goes viral, flailing arms and legs. We watch on repeat, and she pauses the video right when he topples over, all body. Jellyfish, tentacles.

The next video, even shorter: The body doused with water, hauled away by police nationale.

Paula and I cannot bear to read the comments. I kiss the back of her neck.

The synchronized swimming practices begin again in a severely damaged pool. The remaining girls sit hunched together, lock arms, dangle their feet in the cold water. All of the The Men are on the other side, standing and pacing or sitting in the Adirondack chairs, smoking pipes. Some of the The Men are fathers but some of the The Men are simply there to watch. All of the girls have matching black swimming caps on. My father makes a fan out of a piece of paper.

I think about Paula and the curviness of her body, and how beautiful she is even under the film of cold sweat that everyone perpetually carries with them. She says *I wonder where all the animals are. Since the storm, I haven't seen one, not even a bird.*

She lets me put my hands down her underwear until she doesn't. Paula will no longer undress. She has large roots of vein from the inside out. A blistering wound of raw bark, explosion of slivers, connected network. *Let me see*, I beg.

Paula says *no*, a complete sentence. She reaches down her pants and brings up a wooden sliver, uneven toothpick smelling of must.

The Prophet says *This is The End Times*. The Men say *This is War*.

And what they mean by war is simple: Wildness, Violence. Houses are gone or in shambles, Eastern Village no more, deaths, the weather and crop damage, now their daughters, are you kidding me, this is war on the very essence of their beings. The Men talk that The Women were the ones that did the prayin' around there, The Women were the ones who took care, and now The Women are gone, and we gotta figure everything out. The Prophet says *The end times are here. Do you hear me?* The Men shake their heads yes. One man puts both hands to the sky in offering. A flake of ash falls onto the tips of his fingers and balances.

Paula and I sit outside on my front porch with sweaters on. Paula is always chilled to the bone. Rain, sleet, snow, and we remain. I sit closer, lean back on my elbows. I reach out and touch the back of Paula's sweater, so soft. I reach my entire arm around her, rest my fingertips on her side. She tenses. I don't know if it is from my touch, the gesture, or our terrorist older sisters running hand-locked towards the house, shrieking and fighting over an announcement from the government on a red piece of paper.

The piece of paper our terrorist older sisters are fighting over says all infected females must report to The Center for Eradication at once or, if they do not volunteer, they will be taken. *Girls are being sent to internment camps where they are quarantined in domes*, says one terrorist older sister. *We are going to be slaughtered,* says another.

More of our friends get infected:

Each strand of Allison's hair has fallen out, replaced by sprouts petaled in perfect rows, each a different color. Her father buzzes her sprouts down to nubs, but every morning they return.

Callie takes her own life. Her father discovers her hanging in the barn, shoes untied, one fallen from her foot. Her skin covered in dogwood bark.

One friend trapped against two trees, pinned limbs with grapevine leaves as large as heads. Upon first glance, no one is certain if the lump is human—dead or alive. One friend filled with protea, her body weighty with vibrant yellow, magenta spindles, erupting from her shoulders.

Paula tells me before her father left that she walked in on him holding her little sister's head underwater in the bathtub. Paula says her father wept and whispered. He found an aggressive batch of clovers sprouting behind her ear.

Our Friend Jetta Jackson's house is taped off and forbidden. When we break into it, we see we are not the first. The kitchen is a carpet of succulents and cacti. The ceiling of every room hangs with tall grasses, wildflowers. The very last room we enter is occupied with shimmering aspen trees, as if they have always lived here.

Paula & Allison kiss under the arbor of gladiolas in front of Our Friend Jetta Jackson's condemned house and I get mad and blow my cover. I am watching them from across the street behind a dying clematis bush. Allison sighs deeply, loudly, resounding through my body, in my chest, reverberating my head. Allison sighs and it feels as if the entire world sighs, too. Paula yells *oh my god* so I can hear it. I feel so betrayed. I am jealous she is kissing the girl I love. Later, when I run past Allison's house, the men in the hazmat suits are there, taking Allison away.

When I get home, I begin to carve Paula's initials into the tops of my knees. I realize her initials are PAL, she is just my pal. *We aren't anything*, I remember. I take the end of a safety pin and write PAL until blood drips across my leg.

Allison is the first of our friends to be taken to The Center for Eradication. Four men arrive because Allison can no longer hide the buds under her hats and scarves, the nubs a five o'clock shadow of green. One day before swimming practice a nub flowers into an apple blossom and Allison has to pluck it out, her head bleeding enough that she must sit out practice. Now I watch The Men in the yellow hazmat suits seize her and strap her to a gurney, push her into a van.

This is the first time I witness a kidnapping. I am horrified. I run to the van and pound on the sides as it drives away, slamming my fists, slapping my hands.

Today, I do not fight it. There is no use. *They will find you and take you away*, Paula says.

The Center for Eradication is a makeshift quarantined barracks the federal government set up in the wasteland beyond the town for all girls found with vegetation infecting their personage. Everyone is told that The Center for Eradication is a place where treatment is given, where research is diligently being done, where the girls can be taken care of, far away from the epidemic, eliminating the chance of reinfection. The Center for Eradication also lauds itself as an institution dedicated to addressing the post-superstorm, present-war problems of our nation. But really all the girls taken to The Center for Eradication are either put to death immediately upon arrival or used in dangerous studies, unbeknownst to them or The Men. The Center for Eradication wants to figure out how, in a land of total decimation and destruction, these girls manifest vegetation in their bodies. No one is cured. No one walks out alive.

I return from visiting Allison and my father comes home from the revival tent. He changes into a mini-skirt and pink ribbed tank top, a long beaded necklace. We sit at the table in silence for a long while. My father has his toenails painted red, which is why I like my nails painted red, he paints my nails for me, they look professional the other girls say, envious. I do not tell them my father is the artist.

The Prophet has taken over my father, he is a hostage, I say out loud to myself. Hostage Protocol: if you are in a hostage situation or a hostage situation is astir do this in remembrance of me.

I say to my father, *In hostage situations, it's hard to tell who is a hostage and who is the terrorist. For all you know, I could be holding you hostage right now.* I lift my fork and aim it at him.

Stop, he says.

Stop, he says again, and I don't. I wiggle the fork at his nose, *maybe you are a hostage, Dad*, I say, *maybe you are a terrorist.*

The Prophet says, *There are no direct lines between heaven and earth, only hell and earth. And if angels do not come for you, you should expect the devil. The devil comes in many forms. Do not trust anyone in uniform. Do not trust anyone you were raised to believe would protect you. Trust only those who work directly for God. And how do you know who works directly for God? Well, trust and believe. God will speak to you.*

The Men say, *hallelujah, praise, yes sir.*

God will send you a sign, an omen. God will say this Man is of God. These are the dealings of God. Listen to the wisdom. And you, too, will be blessed with the power and glory of the Holy Spirit, can I get an Amen?

The Men say, *Amen, resoundingly.*

Listen to God when he speaks and tells you to follow, and he looks directly at my father, who lowers his head.

A government mandate on a red piece of paper, issued by The Center for Eradication:

All females exhibiting any evidence of vegetation on their person or in their household should be reported immediately.
"Vegetation" includes and is not limited to:

Camellia	Magnolia	Mistletoe	Lily of the Valley
Saguaro Cactus	Louisiana Iris	Indian Blanket	Larkspur
Apple Blossom	White Pine Cone and Tassel	Oregon Grape	Poppy
Queen Anne's Lace	Black-Eyed Susan	Virginia Bluebells	Aster
Rocky Mountain Columbine	Mayflower	Penngift Crown Vetch	Marigold
Mountain Laurel	Apple Blossom	Yellow Jasmine	Hops
Peach Blossom	Dwarf Lake Iris	Pasque Flower	Calendula
Orange Blossom	Pink/White Lady's Slippers	Iris	Chrysanthemum
Wisteria	Hawthorn	Purple Passionflower	Narcissus
Cherokee Rose	Bitterroot	Bluebonnet	Snowdrop
Azalea	Sagebrush	Protea	Daisy
Hawaiian Hibiscus	Purple Lilac	Red Clover	Honeysuckle
Mock Orange	Yucca Flower	American Dogwood	Water Lily
Violet	Rose	Coast Rhododendron	Delphinium
Tulip	Flowering dogwood	Shimmering Aspen	Gladiolus
Wild Prairie Rose	Scarlet Carnation	Carnation	Morning Glory
Sunflower	Large White Trillium	Sweet Pea	Holly
Hollyhock			

II.

In Honor of Escalation: The Pendulum Swings Back

::

Secret From Now On

::

New Beginnings Afoot

UPDATE

A government mandate on a red piece of paper, issued by The Center for Eradication:

 All females exhibiting any evidence of vegetation on their person or in their household should be reported immediately.
"Vegetation" includes and is not limited to:

Camellia	Magnolia	Mistletoe	Lily of the Valley
Saguaro Cactus	Louisiana Iris	Indian Blanket	Larkspur
Apple Blossom	White Pine Cone and tassel	Oregon Grape	Poppy
Queen Anne's Lace	Black-Eyed Susan	Virginia Bluebells	Aster
Rocky Mountain Columbine	Mayflower	Penngift Crown Vetch	Marigold
Mountain Laurel	Apple Blossom	Yellow Jasmine	Hops
Peach Blossom	Dwarf Lake Iris	Pasque Flower	Calendula
Orange Blossom	Pink/White Lady's Slippers	Iris	Chrysanthemum
Wisteria	Hawthorn	Purple Passionflower	Narcissus
Cherokee rose	Bitterroot	Bluebonnet	Snowdrop
Azalea	Sagebrush	Protea	Daisy
Hawaiian Hibiscus	Purple Lilac	Red Clover	Honeysuckle
Mock Orange	Yucca Flower	American Dogwood	Water Lily
Violet	Rose	Coast Rhododendron	Delphinium
Tulip	Flowering dogwood	Shimmering Aspen	Gladiolus
Wild Prairie Rose	Scarlet Carnation	Carnation	Morning Glory
Sunflower	Large White Trillium	Sweet Pea	Holly
Hollyhock			

(Eradication List/Cont.)

Aconitum	Gloriosa Lily	VINING PLANT	Passionflower
Adonis	Grevillea	Algerian Ivy	Purple Passion Plant
Anthrurium	Henbane	Black-Eyed Susan Vine	Star Jasmine
Asclepias	Horse Nettle	Butterfly Pea	Trumpet
Belladonna	Horse-Chestnut	Carolina Jasmine	Wire Vine
Bloodflower	Laceflower	Clematis Snowdrift	
Bloodroot	Maikoa	Clematis 'Anna Karolina'	
Boxwood	Moleplant	Climbing Fig	
Buttercup	Monkshood	Coral Vine	
Butterfly Bush	Nightshade	Cypress Vine	
Scotch Broom	Oleander	Dutchman's Pipe	
Blue Cohosh	Opium	Evergreen Smilax	
Calla Lily	Periwinkle	Fatshedera	
Caladium	Poison Hemlock	Flame Vine	
Clematis	Pokeroot	Golden Trumpet Vine	
Crown Vetch	Sea Anemone	Goldflame Honeysuckle	
Colchicum	Spurge	Honeysuckle	
Datura	Stamonium	Hyacinth Bean	
Dogbane	Toloache	Ivy Geranium	
Elephant Ears	Frangipani	Jackman Clematis	
False Indigo	Lantana	Kenilworth Ivy	
Foxglove	Century Plant	Lotus Vine	

All of our mothers are overseas and suiciding, or coming back honorably discharged and certifiably insane.

The Men are fathers who are unable to separate a daughter from the rest of the women in the world. I understand fathers better because of my father, how kind he is, how wrought with his own grief he is. How Callie could never forget the time her father leaned in for a kiss on her mouth with tongue. She gave into it for a few seconds before pushing him away and running into the house. How she said he covered his face with his hands and cried, slept out in the backyard that night. How Allison's father brushed up against her breasts more than once, pretended it was an accident. How he peeked on her in the bathroom while she showered. How Paula's father, after her mother left for war, began touching her older sister like he touched her mother. Woman of the House.

We start to look for signs. We predicted Allison long before her father found the violets. We saw the violets outside of the house, a small purple in the brown grey hue. Everything in spite of the moisture, in spite of raging water from the skies and the sun that beats down in spite of the high winds, fog and smog that blocks it out, nothing survives, is surviving, is thriving, everything dead. Some days we think being sent to The Center for Eradication would be alright. My father is out of work now that Eastern Village is gone. He pastes an old map of the county on the wall of the living room and circles over and again Eastern Village, the marker circles getting larger, changing colors, black to red, and back to black, blue, as if to resurrect it.

Paula spots a squirrel. It is the first animal we have seen since the storm. We watch the squirrel watching us until we realize the squirrel is dead on the branch. *Who knows how long the body has been there, holding on like that* Paula says.

If the Prophet is right, today I woke up with an omen.
One single blackbird has returned, circling and crying over
the roof of our house. I have no idea how to make it stop.

We wake and the pressure in the air has shifted again. Paula's heart shaped face is caked with blood. Above the eyebrow, lines, much deeper than they should be for her age. The air dry, full of pain, makes our faces bleed. Gums and all, a tooth fell from my mouth. Eventually, a long time from now, Paula's teeth will be extracted except for a back molar that she will pull out with her hands.

New Reports (unofficial):

All of his daughters are soldered together with fan mushrooms coming out of their backs, as if they were born that way, looking like fins from afar, as if they are fishes hung up on a string, mouths together; his twin daughters are fused at the ankles by two saplings; the terrorist older daughter is trapped on her knees as if praying with the most magnificent magnolias you've ever seen swaddling her; his youngest daughter with filaments of cascading green from her head like cables, skewered vertically by a mimosa tree.

Paula & I decide to become blood sisters. We slice open each other's wrists and rub the drips together. We want to brand each other. Paula is uneasy with this idea but I say *I love you and I want your name on me forever*. *You are so stupid*, she says, and hits me on the arm, much harder than I expected. I show her the PAL on my knee, scabbed over. I sketch a backwards P on the inside of my ankle with a needle. No blood comes at first and I panic, maybe the insides of my body have turned into flowers. But eventually, and then all at once.

The syncopated swimming team's numbers dwindle until we are not a team anymore.
Another group of girls are gone as the days of August wear on—
and on—
Every session, our coach pretends the team is getting smaller on purpose.

When our swim coach opens the pool the next morning, there are huge lilies covering the entire surface, the roots connected and attached to the bottom of it where a body floats. Our coach cancels practice indefinitely, never tells our fathers exactly why.

Paula doesn't want anyone to see where her genitals should be is a heliotropic sunflower, losing seeds from the face.

My father dances naked by himself in front of a full-length mirror from his cocaine days. He takes his time putting on nylons, his favorite pleather dress. He lip-synchs to old Phil Spector songs about getting beat but loving that man anyway, or to Cher's "Believe." My father hates the lyric about nothing being strong enough. Occasionally my father wears my mother's clothing, to smell her on his skin, even though he is a much larger bra size than her he quickly finds out, and his hips are narrower, but she must have had a bigger ass than him, he cannot recall how big her ass was. Or was her ass not big at all, she just wore baggy panties? He wonders, what does she even look like?

One morning when my father has his lingerie on, orange heart nipple-pasties underneath fine pink silk, someone knocks on the door. He looks out the window. An official-black-tinted-window-government-car outside. He takes a deep breath, pulls on jeans and a button up dress shirt to cover the lingerie because he knows exactly what this business is about. They don't come to your house unless. He knows with the second persistent knock at the door that his wife is dead.

As news of our mothers reach us, Paula & I cry, both for different reasons. My mother has died. Paula's mother is returning, certifiable and honorable.

Paula's mother is alive. She is obsessed with the current state of affairs. She joins support groups, relief efforts. She cleans her home top to bottom. She grieves her dead husband, her two daughters. She never lets Paula out of her sight. She has a hard time speaking, has a hard time concentrating on one thing for long. She wakes up screaming in the night.

My father, in my mother's cashmere sweater, her string of black pearls, her black, shiny, kitten heels, holds the folded American flag in his lap. A certificate of bereavement signed by the President in front of him on the table.

Would she like to be buried in a military cemetery? Would she like a military funeral? he asks me. I start to cry.

I am staying the night with Paula and she says *I want you to see.* She lifts the bottom of her nightgown to reveal knotty, splintered wood. Flakes of her skin like rind, ribbed and curled. Her thighs covered with mosses. I see the tiniest patch of hens and chickens where her clitoris once was. She says, *There was a sunflower there but I cut it. Does anyone know,* I ask. *Tell me who knows.* She looks away.

Paula is taken. I pretended to sleep through the commotion. Her nightgown is on the chair when I open my eyes.

Inside The Center for Eradiation: There are girls hooked up to breathing machines; girls gasping like fishes; girls in wheelchairs with their insides showing; girls with bones of rotting stems; a room that contains a girl whose head is a hydrangea bush. There are girls walking upright; girls walking twisted from the knees or torso or clavicle. Girls with tree bark faces. There are girls with chests and backs of buds and petals, death blossoms stinking. There is a girl who no longer has fingers but green leaves that move like snakes. There are girls hooked to machines, no longer allowed visitors. There are girls who have already been forgotten about in such a short amount of time. There are girls whose bodies are hairy and pointy, smooth and silky, thorny, bushy, fragile, full of holes as if caterpillars are eating away at them. A girl with a bouquet of flowers in the center of her ribs, pushing out like a baby at full term. A girl with Tiffany blue petals as pupils. Girls with flower heads, deadheaded, as if in the final season harvest all over their bodies. A girl who vomits whole devil's broomsticks, triple headed branches and all.

So many girls, instead of genitals, instead of a clit or an opening, instead of an anus proper, have flowers, have roots, have bark, have green buds, heads in season, so many have a forest, a new kind of incurable, transmitted disease.

When I enter Paula's room at The Center for Eradication, the bed has been removed. There are remnants of hard stalks of Queen Anne's Lace surrounding where the bed once was, wheel trails through the door of clippings into the hallway. The TV is on, a dog show, waves applause. The white board says who Paula's nurse is, what time of day her meds are, the amount of pain she is in. There is no nurse name or time of day for meds, only a 5 in the box for pain, which is pretty good considering, I think.

I am told by a blue-haired nurse that the last time they saw Paula, a Queen Anne's bud had sprouted from the back of her right knee. She was airlifted somewhere else this morning. I imagine the doctors cutting Paula's leg open to find a stem instead of a bone.

During the storm, in the middle of it, after we ran inside and the electricity clapped out, before we moved downstairs behind a mattress as we were instructed to do, we decided to go upstairs and watch through the bow picture window, the only window that we couldn't reach not boarded up, we sat on the couch, and Paula grabbed my hand and held it while we watched the streetlight get lifted and thrown as if someone had back-handed it. If it had been the other direction, it would have crashed through the window and killed us. And then everything went silent. Just like that, the storm is done, we naively thought.

Today when I am back from The Center for Eradication, I am numb. I sit on the couch by myself. The sky outside is nebulous with ash. I have not seen a clear sky since the storm. It is light outside but there is no sun. Everything is brown except for our yard which matches the sky in color and I cannot tell where our grey lawn and the grey sky begin and end.

My heart has grown thorns. The rain comes again, and my instinct is to panic and hide. To board the windows. Make a protective barrier. To say good-bye, in my head, to everything and everyone I have loved and known. I love you and see you next time. I reach for Paula's hand in the night. I leave my hand behind me while I am sleeping in case Paula wants it to touch her but she is not there. Her whole family is gone. I walk past their house in the morning and the entire top of the house has caved in under the weight of what looks like millions of orchids. I swear I see birds scattering from the exposed rubble, but when I approach the house there is nothing.

The Prophet asks my father to speak with him one night after the revival. He says, *I have something to show you. I think you are going to like it. Here, read this. I await your feedback, brother.*

My father opens the envelope to a set of extremely rough prototypes on yellow legal paper in blue ball point ink, tracts for daughters. Folded vertically, the title: Your Mother is At War, How You Can Help Your Father.

First page: Your Mother Is At War, So It Is Your Godly Duty To Help Your Father With…

Second page: …With Whatever He May Need: various chores such as cleaning, laundry, preparing meals, groceries…
…And, Since Your Mother Is At War, He May Need You To: sleep in bed with him, touch him where he wants to be touched, let him touch you. God Says, Honor Your Father.

Third page: …And, Since Your Mother Is At War, And You Are Afraid To Let Your Father Touch You, Go See The Prophet And He Will Help You. You Must Honor Your Father (with a crude drawing of a man with his hand on the knees of a pigtailed child, sitting on a church pew).

By the time my father finishes the third page, he feels sick. He crumples the tracts into a ball in his hand. *We will leave tomorrow*, he says.

In the morning, my father sits in the back of the tent. The Prophet enters the stage from behind the choir pews.

Have you done what I have asked of you, brother? The Prophet asks.

Yes, of course, my father says, looking past The Prophet at the crucifix, Jesus' face in need of mercy.

My father bows his head with the The Men. He says all the words that he is expected to say, amen, hallelujah, calls everyone brother. We are going to leave in a few short hours. He opens his eyes to deadlock with The Prophet. My father shakes the sweat from his hair, clears his throat, itches his pantyhose underneath his heavy work jeans.

My father & I make our way down the gravel drive to the revival tent. Through the blur of the trees, everything looks as though it is bloated.

My father says *We have to get out of here.* I do not understand his urgency, but I do understand my own. There is nothing left for me. Take me away, good father.

Our car is lightly packed. We have left most everything behind. I took a picture of the front of the house, everything boarded up except the bow window, X 2 in spray paint, meaning Paula and I were alive, holding hands behind a mattress.

I see Paula in the window. I never see Paula again.

UPDATE

A government mandate on a red piece of paper, issued by The Center for Eradication:

All females exhibiting any evidence of vegetation on their person or in their household should be reported immediately. "Vegetation" includes and is not limited to:

Abelia	Amaryllis	Azalea
Aconitum	American Dune Grass	Baby Blue Eyes
Adam's Needle	American Persimmon	Baby's Breath
Adnia	Anemone	Bachelor Buttons
Adonis	Angel Wing Begonia	Bacopa
African Corn Lily	Angel's Trumpets	Balloon Flower
African Moon	Angelica	Bamboo
African Tulip	Anise Magnolia	Banana Shrub
Agapanthus	Annual Delphinium	Banana Yucca
Agave	Anomathe	Barberry
Aleppo Pine	Antelope Horns	Barberton
Alfalfa	Anthrurium	Basil Flower
Algerian Ivy	Apple Blossom	Basket of Gold
Allium	Arikury Palm	Bat Face Plant
Almond	Arum	Bat Flower
Alpine Aster	Asclepius	Bear's Breeches
Alipinia	Ashe Magnolia	Beard Tongue
Alum Root	Asparagus Fern	Beautyberry
Alyssum	Aster	Beautybrush
Amaranthus	Avens	Bee Balm Flower

(Eradication List/Cont.)

Bloodflower
Bloodroot
Bloody Butcher
Bloody Cranesbill
Bloom
Blue Cardinal Flower
Blue Carpet
Blue Chalksticks
Blue Clumping Wheatgrass
Blue Cohosh

Blue Dawn Flower
Blue Jacaranda
Blue Palo Verde
Blue Star
Blue Torch
Blue Vervain
Blue Passionflower
Bluebeard
Bluebell
Bluebonnet

Bog Rosemary
Boronia
Bottlebrush
Bougainville
Bouvardia
Box Bedstraw
Boxwood
Brass Buttons
Brazilian Passionflower
Breadfruit

Begonia
Belladonna
Bellflower
Bells of Ireland
Benjamin Fig
Bermuda Grass
Bethlehem Sage
Big Betony
Big Cone Pine
Big Periwinkle

Bigroot Geranium
Birch
Bird's Eye
Bird's Nest Fern
Birds of Paradise
Birdsfoot Trefoil
Bishop's Flower
Bishop's Hate
Bishop's Weed
Bitter Ground

Bitterroot
Black Walnut
Black-Eyed Susan
Black-Eyed Susan Vine
Blackthorn
Blanket Flower
Blazing Star
Bleeding Heart
Bleeding Heartwine
Blood Lily

Bronze Sedge
Buddha Belly Plant
Bugleweed
Burning Bush
Busy Lizzie
Buttercup
Butterfly Bush
Butterfly Milkweed
Butterfly Pea
Butternut

Cabbage Palm
Caladium
Calathea
Calendula
California Poppy
Calla Lily
Callery Pear
Camellia
Campanula
Cana Palm

Candytuft
Canterbury Bells
Capa Rose
Cape Primrose
Caper
Caraway Thyme
Cardinal Flower
Carnation
Carolina Jasmine
Carpet Bugle

(Eradication List/Cont.)

Cast Iron Plant
Castor Bean
Catalpa
Catasetum
Catmint
Cattleya
Celosia
Century Plant
Checkerbloom

Cherry Blossom
Chervil
Chestnut Oak
Chia
Chicory
Chilean Jasmine
China Fir
China Fleece Vine
China Wood Oil Tree

Chinese Fan Palm
Chinese Houses
Chinese Lanterns
Chives
Chocolate Cosmos
Chocolate Flower
Choke Cherries
Christmas Bells
Christmas Rose
Chysanthemum

Cigar Flower
Cigar Plant
Cigarette Plant
Cineraria
Cinnamon Fern
Cinquefoil
Clasping Coneflower
Clematis
Clematis Snowdrift
Climbing Fig

Cloudland Rhododendron
Clover
Clubhair Mariposa Lily
Cockleblur
Cockscomb
Cocoplum
Colchicum
Columbine
Common Boneset
Common Silverbell

Cone Flower
Constania
Contra Costa Goldfields
Coolibah
Coontie
Coral Bells
Coral Honeysuckle
Coral Vine
Coralberry
Corn Cockles

Corn Plant
Cornflower
Cosmos
Cotoneaster
Cottage Pink
Coyote Bush
Crabapple
Crabgrass
Cranberry
Cranesbill

Crapemyrtle
Cream Wild Indigo
Creeping Charlie
Creeping Juniper
Crimson Clover
Crocus
Croton
Crown Vetch
Cryptopodium
Cupid's Dart

Curly Top Sedge
Cyad
Cyclamen
Cypress Vine
Daffodil
Dahlia
Daisy
Dame's Rocket
Darley Dale Heath
Date Palm

(Eradication List/Cont.)

Datura
Dead Nettle
Delphinium
Dense Blazing Star
Desert Olive
Deutzia
Dewberries
Dianthus
Diascia
Didiscus

Dill
Dog's Mercury
Dogbane
Dogwood Tree
Downy Serviceberry
Downy Thorn Apple
Draba
Dragon Lily
Dragon Spruce
Dusty Miller

Dutchman's Pipe
Dymondia
Easter Cactus
Eastern Cottonwood
Eastern Pasque Flower
Eastern Redbud
Ebony Blackbeard
Ebony Spleenwort
Echinops
Edelweiss

Edging Lobelia
Eggplant
Elderberry
Elephant Ears
Encyclia
English Daisy
Eryngium
Etlingera
Eucalyptus
Evening Primrose

Evergreen Smilax
Fairy Wings
False Aralia
False Indigo
False Solomon's Seal
False Spirea
Fan Flower
Farewell-to-Spring
Fatshedera
Feather Celosia

Feverfew
Fiddleleaf Fig
Field Wood-Rush
Finetooth Holly
Finger Poppy Mallow
Fingerleaf Rodgers Flower
Firebrush
Firecracker Flower
Flame Grass
Flame of the Woods

Flame Tip
Flame Vine
Flamegold
Flat Sea Holly
Flatwoods Plum
Flax
Flax Lily
Fleabane
Florida Anise
Florida Bully

Floss Flower
Flowering Onion
Flowering Tobacco
Foamflower
Forget-Me-Not
Formosa Sweet Gum
Fortune's Sweet Olive
Fountain Grass
Fox Red Curley Sage
Foxglove

Frangipani
Franklin Tree
Freesia
Fuchsia
Garden Roses
Gardenia
Gas Plant
Gay Feather
Gentian Speedwell
Gentiana

(Eradication List/Cont.)

Georgia Bush Honeysuckle	Grevillea	Holly
Geranium	Ground Ivy	Hollyhock
Gerberas	Ground Morning Glory	Honeysuckle
Ghost Flower	Hair Grass	Hoop and Petticoat Daffodil
Ghost Orchid	Hairyfruit Chewstick	Hopbrush
Giant Dumbcane	Hakone Grass	Hops
Giant Tree Yucca	Harry Lauder's Walking Stick	Horned Violet
Gibraltar Campion	Hart's Tongue Fern	Horse Nettle
Ginger	Hat Palm	Horse-Chestnut
Ginkgo	Hawaiian Hibiscus	Horsemint
Gladiolus	Hawthorn	Horseradish
Glaucous-Leaf Greenbriar	Hazelnut	Hosta
Globe Gilla	Heart Leaf Philodendron	Hot Lips Sage
Globe Thistle	Heartleaf Saxifrage	Houseleek
Glory Lily	Heath	Houttuynia
Glory of the Snow	Heather	Hurrican Palm
Glorybower	Heavenly Bamboo	Hyacinth
Gloxinia	Hedgehog Agave	Hyacinth Bean
Goat's Rue	Helen's Flower	Hyacinth Orchid
Godetia	Heliconia	Hydrangea
Golden Bells	Helitrope	Hypericum
Golden Shower	Hellebore	Hyssop
Golden Trumpet Vines	Hemigraphis	Impatiens
Golden Wattle	Henbane	Indigo
Goldenrod	Henbit	Interrupted Fern
Goldflame Honeysuckle	Henry's Lily	Iris
Grape Hyacinth	Hepatica	Irish Moss
Grass of the Dew	Hesper Palm	Ironweed
Greater Celandine	Higan Cherry	
Green Carpet	Homan Holly	

(Eradication List/Cont.)

Island Oak	Kenilworth Ivy	Lawson's Cypress
Italian Cypress	Kentucky Bluegrass	Leadwort
Ivory Pineapple	Kentucky Coffee Tree	Leatherleaf
Ivy Geranium	Kerria	Leatherwood
Jacaranda	Key Thatch Palm	Lemon Balm
Jack in the Pulpit	King Sago Palm	Lemon Bottlebrush
Jack Pine	Kiwi	Lemon Grass
Jackman Clematis	Knife Acacia	Lemon Mint
Jacob's Ladder	Knotweed	Lemonade Berry
Jacob's Rod	Koki'o	Lenten Rose
Jade Tree	Koutruk Lei	Leopard's Bane
Jade Vine	Kurrajong	Lesser Celandine
Jamestown Weed	Lacebark Pine	Lewisia
Japanese Alpine Cherry	Laceflower	Licorice Plant
Japanese Yew	Lady Fern	Lilac
Jasmine	Lady Palm	Lilium
Jewel Plant	Lady Tulip	Lily
Joannis Palm	Lady's Mantle	Lily of the Nile
Joe Pye Weed	Ladybells	Lily of the Valley
Johnny Jump-Up	Ladyslipper	Lilyturf
Joseph's Coat	Laelia	Linden
Joshua Tree	Lamb's Ear	Lion's Ear
Juniper	Lantana	Lion's Tail Flower
Juniper's Beard	Larch	Lisianthus
Kafir Lily	Larkspur	Lithodora
Kalanchoe	Lavadin	Lobelia
Kalimeris	Lavender	Lobstercla
Kalm St. Johnswort	Lavender Cotton	Locust
Kamchatka Bugbane	Lavender Globe Lily	Loosestrife
Kangaroo Paw	Lavender Mist Meadow Rue	Lotus

(Eradication List/Cont.)

Lotus Vine
Lovage
Love in a Mist
Love Lies Bleeding
Lungwort
Lupin
Lydia Broom
Macarthur Palm
Madagascar Dragon Tree
Madagascar Jasmine

Madam Galen's Trumpet Vine
Madrone
Madwort
Magnolia
Maiden Grass
Maiden Pink
Maikoa
Maltese Cross
Manchurian Cherry

Maple
Marigold
Malberry
Marvel of Peru
Masterwort
Matilija Poppy
Maxillaria
Mayapple
Mayflower
Mazus

Morning Glory
Moss
Moss Rose
Moth Orchid
Mountain Bluet
Mountain Fleece
Mountain Laurel
Mube
Mullein
Mum

Musas
Muscadine Grape
Muscari
Naked Lady Flowers
Nanking Cherry
Nannyberry
Naranjilla
Narrowleaf Cattail
Nasturtium
Natal Plum

Needle Juniper
Neillia
Nemesia
New England Aster
Nicotiana
Nigella
Nightshade
Ninebark
Nippon Spirea

Meadow Cranesbill
Meadow Sage
Meadowsweet
Mealycup Sage
Mediterranean Pink Heather
Melampodium
Mescal
Mexican Buckeye
Mexican Bush Sage
Mexican Hat

Mexican Poppy
Middlemist Red
Milk Vetch
Milkweed
Million Bells
Mimosa
Mint
Mioga Ginger
Missouri Evening Primrose
Mistflower

Moleplant
Mondo Grass
Money Plant
Monkey Flower
Monkey Puzzle
Monkeypod
Monkshood
Montbretia
Moon Grass
Moor Grass

85

(Eradication List/Cont.)

Nolana
Nootka Rose
Norfolk Island
Oak
Oak Fern
Oak Leaf Ivy
Oak-Leaf Hydrangea
Oat Grass
Obedient Plant
Oconee Bells

Octopus Tree
Odorless Mock Orange
Okame Zasa
Oklahoma Rose
Old Man Palm
Oleander
Oleaster
Olive
Opium
Orange Blossom

Orange Coneflower
Orange Jasmine
Orange Sneezeweed
Orange Star Plant
Orange Wallflower
Orchid
Oregano
Oregon Grape
Oriental Poppy
Ornamental Onion

Ornamental Pear
Orris Root
Osage Orange
Osteospermum
Ox-Eye
Oxalis
Oyster Plant
Pacaya
Pagoda Dogwood
Painted Daisy

Painted Fingernail Bromeliad
Painter's Palette
Palm
Palm Sedge
Pampas Grass
Panakenake
Panicle Hydrangea
Pansy
Paper Birch
Paperbark Maple

Parlor Palm
Parrot's Beak
Parrot's Feather
Parry's Pinyon
Parsley
Partrinia
Pasque Flower
Passionflower
Patchoa Flower
Patridge Pea

Pawpaw
Peace Lily
Peach Leafed Bellflower
Pearlbush
Pearlwort
Peony
Peppermint
Periwinkle
Persian Buttercup
Persian Ivy

Peruvian Lily
Petunia
Philadelphia Flaebane
Phlox
Pieris
Pig Squeak
Pigweed
Pimento Palm
Pincussion
Pineapple Guava

Pineapple Lily
Pineapple Sage
Pink Breath-of-Heaven
Pink Lady's Slipper
Pink Quill
Pink Wild Bean
Pink/White Lady's Slipper
Pinwheel
Pipevine

(Eradication List/Cont.)

Plantain
Platycodon
Plumbago
Pocketbook Flower
Poinsetta
Poison Hemlock
Poison Sumac
Pokeroot
Pokeweed
Poplar Tree

Poppy
Portulaca
Post Oak
Pot Marigold
Potato Vine
Pothos Plant
Powderpuff
Prairie Gentian
Prairie Smoke
Primrose

Primula
Privet Tree
Protea
Purple Lilac
Purple Love Grass
Purple Passion Plant
Purslane
Pussy Willow
Quaking Aspen
Queen Anne's Lace

Queen Lily Ginger
Queen of the Prairie
Queen Palm
Queen Victoria Century Plant
Queen's Crapemyrtle
Queensland Palm
Quince
Rabbit Tale Grass
Rabbit's Foot Fern
Rabbitbush

Raffia Palm
Rain of Gold
Ranunculus
Raspberry
Rattlesnake Master
Red Clover
Red Edge Dracaena
Red Fescue
Red Fox
Red Hot Poker

Rex
Rhododendron
Ribbon Grass
Rice Paper Plant
Rock Rose
Rockcress
Rocket Larkspur
Rose
Rose Campion
Rose Mallee

Scilla
Scotch Bloom
Scotch Heather
Sea
Sea Anemone
Sea Buckthorn
Sea Grape
Sea Holly
Sea Lavender
Sea Oats

Sea Pink
Sedge
Sego Lily
Self Heal
Senegal Date Palm
Sensitive Fern
Sensitive Plant
September Flower
Serissa
Shamrock

Shasta Daisy
Shooting Star
Showy Dewflower
Shrimp Plant
Siam Tulip
Siberian Bugloss
Siebold
Silk Oak
Silver Lace
Silverberry

(Eradication List/Cont.)

Simpson's Stopper
Singapore Orchid
Sloe
Smoke Tree
Smooth Blue Aster
Snake Plant
Snapdragon
Sneezeweed
Sneezewort

Snow in Summer
Snowball
Snowbell
Snowberry
Snowdrop
Snowy Woodrush
Soapweed
Soapwort
Society Garlic
Solomon's Seal

Sonchus
Sophora
Sophornitella
Sophronitis
Sourweed
Speedwell
Spider Flower
Spider Lily
Spiderwort
Spiked Speedwell

Rose of Sharon
Rose of Turtlehead
Rosemary
Roisinweed Sunflower
Rough Horsetail
Rudbeckia
Rue Anemone
Russian Olive
Rusty Foxglove
Ryegrass

Saffron
Sage
Sagebrush
Sago Palm
Salal
Salvia
Sampaguita
Sand Dollar Cactus
Sandwort
Santa Barbara

Sapphire Flower
Sargent
Sasakatoon Serviceberry
Sassafras
Satin Leaf
Saucer Magnolia
Saw-Tooth Sunflower
Saxifrage
Scabious
Scarlet Sterculia

Spiral Flag
Spirea
Spotted Bellflower
Spotted Dead Nettle
Spray Carnation
Spring Beauty
Spring Snowflake
Spring Starflower
Spring Vetch
Spurge

Squaw Weed
Squill
St. John's Wort
Star Jasmine
Star of Bethlehem
Stargazer Lily
Statice
Stephanotis
Stock
Stonecress

Stonecrop
Stramonium
Strawflower
Sugarbush
Sulphur Cosmos
Sundrop
Sunflower
Sunshine Palm
Swamp Mallee
Swan River Daisy

(Eradication List/Cont.)

Sweet Crabapple
Sweet Flag
Sweet Pea
Sweet Potato Vine
Sweet William
Switchgrass
Tailflower
Talinum
Tall Coneflower
Tall Speedwell

Tam Juniper
Tamarisk
Tangerine
Taro
Tartarian Dogwood
Tassle Fern
Tea Oil Camellia
Tea Tree Camellia
Texas Bluebonnet
Thanksgiving Cactus

Thatch Palm
Thistle
Thrift
Thyme
Tickseed
Tidy Tips
Tigerlily
Toadflax
Toloache
Tomato

Toothache Plant
Torch Ginger
Trachelium
Transvaal Daisy
Trapper's Tea
Treasure Flower
Trillium
Triteleia
Tritonia
Trumpet

Tuberose
Tulip
Tung-Oil Tree
Tutsan
Twinspur
Two Row Stonecrop
Umbrella Grass
Umbrella Magnolia
Umbrella Plant
Uncarina

Urn Plant
Ussurian Pear
Utah Juniper
Vanda
Vanhoutte Spirea
Veltheimia
Velvet Leaf
Venus Slipper
Venus's Car
Verbena

Vernal Witchhazel
Veronica
Viburnum
Victorian Box
Vinca Rosea
Vine Lilac
Vine Maple
Virgin's Bower
Virginia Bluebells
Virginia Pepperweed

Virginia Sweetspire
Vitex
Waldsteinia
Wall Rockcress
Wallflower
Walter
Wandflower
Warty Barberry
Washington Hawthorn

Water Birch
Water Hyacinth
Water Lettuce
Water Lily
Water Oak
Water Tupelo
Watermelon Peperomia
Waxflower
Waxleaf Privet
Wayfaring Tree

(Eradication List/Cont.)

Wedelia
Weeping Bottlebrush
Weeping Weigela
Western Hemlock
Whirling Butterflies
White Alder
White Clover
White Dead Nettle
White Pine Cone and Tassel
White Root

Whitebark Magnolia
Whitlow Grass
Wild Carrot
Wild Comfrey
Wild Date Palm
Wild Ginger
Wild Lime
Wild Onion
Wild Raisin
Wild Strawberry

Windflower
Winged Everlasting
Winter Daphne
Wintercreeper
Wire Vine
Wishbone Flower
Wisteria
Witch Alder
Witch Hazel
Wood Sorrel

Woodbine Honeysuckle
Woodland Lettuce
Woodrush
Wormwood
Woundwort
Yarrow
Yellow Corydalis
Yellow Jessamine
Yellow Sedge
Yew

Zebra Grass
Zinnia

Katie Jean Shinkle is the author of three full-length books and four chapbooks, most recently *There Are So Many Things That Beg You For Love* (damaged goods press, 2017) and *The Arson People* (Civil Coping Mechanisms, 2015). Other work can be found in or is forthcoming from *New South*, *Washington Square Review*, *Ninth Letter*, *Booth*, and elsewhere. She is an Assistant Professor of English at Central State University in Wilberforce, Ohio.

www.ingramcontent.com/pod-product-compliance
Lightning Source LLC
Chambersburg PA
CBHW021447080526
44588CB00009B/723